Poor-Mouth
Jubilee

THE TUPELO MASTERS SERIES

* Also available as audio books at www.tupelopress.org.

POOR-MOUTH JUBILEE

POEMS BY MICHAEL CHITWOOD

Michael Chitwood (signature)

Tupelo Press
North Adams, Massachusetts

Library of Congress Cataloging-in-Publication Data
Chitwood, Michael.
Poor-mouth jubilee : poems / Michael Chitwood. – 1st paperback ed.
    p. cm. – (The Tupelo masters series)
ISBN 978-1-932195-89-7 (pbk. : alk. paper)
I. Title.
PS3553.H535P66 2010
811'.54–dc22

                        2010

Cover and text designed by Josef Beery.
Cover photograph: "All day community sing, Pie Town, New Mexico," June
1940, by Russell Lee (1903–1986). From the Farm Security Administration /
Office of War Information Photograph Collection (U.S. Library of Congress),
LC-DIG-fsa-8a28924.

First paperback edition, October 2010.
13 12 11 10   5 4 3 2 1

Printed in the United States on FSC-certified recycled paper, with electricity
from wind energy.

Tupelo Press
P.O. Box 1767, North Adams, Massachusetts 01247
Telephone: (413) 664–9611 / Fax: (413) 664–9711
editor@tupelopress.org / www.tupelopress.org

Tupelo Press is an award-winning independent literary press that publishes
fine fiction, non-fiction, and poetry in books that are a joy to hold as well as
read. Tupelo Press is a registered 501(c)3 non-profit organization, and we rely
on public support to carry out our mission of publishing extraordinary work
outside the realm of large commercial publishers. Financial donations are
welcome and are tax deductible.

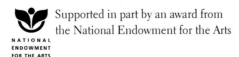 Supported in part by an award from
the National Endowment for the Arts

NATIONAL
ENDOWMENT
FOR THE ARTS

for

Steve Henry Sink

who made every day count

CONTENTS

PROOF

THE DEER

I am being prayed for. The deer
appear across the road. They seem to
drift from the understory, alert, ready to
startle.

When they cross the road to come
into my yard, they have the mincing
steps on the macadam of women in heels
on the icy sidewalks outside a church.
Someone is sick.

As autumn deepens their coats will
darken, go grayer so that they will blend
with the slates and pewters of winter
trunks.

They are creatures of listening.

Their hunger brings them here.

NEVER TAKE YOUR OWN ADVICE

Don't Complain

I would like to know the dumb joy
of trees, their misspelled love notes,
*b*s and *d*s facing the wrong way
and still they are standing.

I think they like their feet wet.
They can stand in a sob all day
and in the evening not think once about lumber.

They invite bees to tickle their genitalia
and bees oblige.

They carelessly grow the fruit of knowledge
and will let it rot to a fare-thee-well.

Some have winged seeds
that clot the mouth of the downspout
and make a black spunk so rich
one or two will live.

WORK AT YOUR MARRIAGE

Newlyweds on the honeymoon trip,
they are trying to get
from one set of ruins to the next.
There were no double berths.
He took the top.
Now they are three feet apart.
Neither sleeping.

They are perfectly still,
hurtling over the landscape.

NEVER TAKE YOUR OWN ADVICE

Two male cardinals are having at it
in the front yard.
They collide in mid-air, two red fists.
When they take a break
and rest in separate dogwood trees,
their taunts and threats
are rendered in the sweet liquid notes
of pebbles plinking into water,

reminding me of yesterday at dusk
when I walked out to the pond.
A chevron of geese flew over silently,
no blustering honks,
just the whirring of their wings
which they continued to employ
because I was there.

Take Comfort Where You Can

Not for nothing
are we given at least as much
sense as God gave a goose,
which we have no access to, sensewise.
We don't speak goose
nor recognize what body language
there may be in a body
which is mostly neck and dollop.
But down, now there is something
to build dreams on.
We have recourse
and in the morning the feathered snow
will have come and closed the roads.
Linger. Leave off.

BE GOOD TO YOURSELF

Kinda fresh in vertigos
I got back into bed
after my glass of juice.
The sun slatted itself
through the louvered window.
A wren was chirping his ass off
for home and health.
At least that's how I heard it.
Early March,
I thought of the forsythia
about to go yellow
along all its whips.

MAKE EACH DAY COUNT

On the way to the memorial service
it started to snow,
blanking our view of the moon's afternoon ghost,
cold clock so white it was blue.

The speakers' voices caught.
They had to pause to continue.
Beneath the lauds,
the talk of deep friendship
and a life well-lived,
we heard the rasp
of the maintenance crew's shovels,
having had to come in on a Saturday.

SELF-HELP

SELF-HELP

Great-Great-Grandpa Self,
the yawp is loosed.
We are talk.

In the streets, in bedrooms,
in elevators, in the great stadiums,
in our cars as we plunge into sunlight,
we are not without voices,
saying and said to.

We are the great cast of one
and the great audience of one.

Last night
as I worried for my health
and didn't sleep,

I heard the frantic *whos*
of the Great Horned Owl,
his rapid love song

or a warning
to other horned owls.
My neighbors heard it too

if they worried for my health.

A young woman is crying into her phone.
She is in the park across from the medical center.
This could be coincidence.

Some Britney or Tiffany.
Her parents divorced when she was a child.
She did well enough in school

and sucked off a boy she'd just met
on a hotel balcony in Florida.
Has she just been told she has breast cancer?

She's dressed for business.
Was the doctor's appointment on her lunch break?
Her head is slightly bowed

to create a little privacy.
But we can see she is crying.
Perhaps we should go over

and sit with her
and hold her hand,
whoever we are, so totally random.

Great-Great-Grandpa Self,
you say in your great poem,
  "You (meaning me with your book in my hand) *shall no longer take*
  things at second or third hand, nor look through the eyes of the dead
  (no comment), *nor feed on the specters in books,/ You shall not look*
  through my eyes either, nor take things from me,/ You shall listen to
  all sides and filter them from yourself (meaning myself, with your book
  in my hand)."

The wall speeds. It hurtles,
but its speed is constant

so it seems to be still.
On the other side

the owl huffs and hoots before dawn,
then the smaller birds trill,

the vine curls its come-hither tendril,
bees bump blossoms

and my love yawns, stretches,
her nipples pressed to her taut shirt.

◈

For a long time after the diagnosis
I wasn't myself,
but I was selfish.

◈

At the Chapel of the Chained Ankles
people have left pictures

of loved ones they want healed
and notes in begging cursive.

They take away dirt in vials,
so much dirt it has to be replenished.

At night the priests
bring in bucketfuls from elsewhere on the grounds,

sacred dirt is sacred dirt they reason.
All day the grieving dust collects dust.

Heal us, Lord, they pray,
You who created us into sickness.

In the tiny room with the dirt floor they crowd.
They must shuffle as though shackled.

We are talk
and the wall speeds.

The self rides,
a woman asleep on an airplane,

peaceful, chuffing breaths, hurtling.
Outside the skin

the mile of plunge.

The sheen of rain on asphalt,
the surface of puddles,

rivers like roads through landscapes,
the shiny skin of cars,

windows when it's dark out,
the flat dull blades of case knives

and the bowls of spoons
and the silver sides of napkin dispensers

and, of course, mirrors.
Some people decorate with them.

All over the house,
we flash and walk through.

From the front porch
I can hear the rumble of voices on the radio inside.

It's a talk show, muffled argument.
I can't tell what they are saying

but hear the emotional pitch, the ire,
the misunderstanding of history, culture,

you, no you, so much at stake
in getting it said,

as it was not those summer mornings
when I would wake in the tent

and hear the canvas-buffered talk
as they cooked breakfast outside.

Low chat punctuated with bird calls.
All that made me I heard.

The wall speeds.
In the marriage bed

it flies.
At the cradle of the newborn

it sings with quickness.

In the handshake
it rushes.

It's what's between us,
our connection.

Health to the self,
its ease,

lying on a chaise,
Saturday afternoon,

the mowing done
and the pruning,

lattice of the screen
making a shadow lace on the body.

17

THREE DOGS AS THE FIGURE OF DEATH

They have found the sunny spot in the yard.
They are in relation, triangulate.
They are like loaves rising, their warm bodies in ferment.

Here Here and Here
The truth is
Say what you will

I see the one most forward as the prayer of the other two.
Fur is its own reward.
They can smell me thinking.

CROWS AS THE FIGURE OF DISEASE

They are perched on the pewter winter branches of the poplar.

Periodically, they caw.

They recoil from their song like pistols firing.

We say small arms. Gunmetal, blue-black.

They would feed on a body, given the opportunity.

They sail to the ground and walk like priests in their cassocks.

Clever, they can't be gotten rid of.

Lifting, back to the tree,

they are for an instant an eighth note, then a quarter.

To sing them would require only a sip of air.

VISITING TOM

The fields empty for miles, no hills.
It was like God was rushing at you,

the big winter nothingness of it.
The motorcycle leaned jauntily

on its kick stand, his one happiness.
Speed and risk gathered in his wrist.

We ate at a fly-speck diner
where I was recognized as a stranger.

The landscape was going-down-and-not-
coming-up gray, the bare trees, clouds,

the glowering sky and feeble sun smear,
all gray. I told Tom his helmet

on the table was thinking of leaving.
He said yeah he'd heard that too.

That he was able to live. That he
later turned the truck off, took the hose

out of the tailpipe. That he made it
out, to Greece for God's sake. That. That.

Fourth Hour of
the Afternoon

Humidity like gauze tape on the skin.
Butterflies have come to the butterfly bush.
I like the way that sentence walks,

foot-testing the rocks for a solid way across.
Cicadas torque their gear boxes,
and North Carolina is coming about,

its troll motors chuffing and dropping rainbow splatters
on the gray waters upon which we slide.
Always a royal formality stands up

when we try to utter the unutterable.
It was ever thus, those lice-ridden Lords
translating the altar blood of fatted calves.

A cold front is bringing the Pentecost
to the pine tops. There's a shiver in that herd,
ozone sharp as a whiff of hot tin.

You can see the rain coming, cowled,
head down, hiking steady with its crystal
prayer beads worried in wordless prayer.

IN GOD WE TRUST

FEDERAL RESERVE NOTES

I ain't broke but I'm badly bent
Everybody loves those dead presidents
—Little Walter

❧ *Single*

Mythic tissue,
be legal and tender,

a telegram proclaiming
Washington's ardor.

"In God We Trust
all others pay cash"

yuks the stitch work
below a framed one

above the register.
A sawbuck heehaw.

A bet against a donut,
earned by another day,

or short by 24 hours,
this honest ticket

has four eyes
if you count the eagle's,

speaks Latin
and on payday translates

to takeout and a video.
The guy with the caption

comes in handy for coffee.
A little page from our Book

of the Dead. It's called
circulation and currency,

embossed with the past.
All alone and crumpled

it's good for a bad cigar
or mailing two letters.

Laced with cocaine
and lining the collection plate,

hand to hand like combat
or courtship, it adds up.

All debts, public or private.
Do you love me?

Circle one.

Yes or no?

⚘ *To Lincoln on the Five*

I think you've been pacing
or were sitting askew in a chair,
your stork legs over the arm,
and now you've come to the little window
to see what moonlight there might be,
how the magnolia leaves glint in it.

The particular copy I have is faded
from hours in the archives
of a scuffed leatherette purse
or the front pocket of a pair of jeans.

I think you like it best alone there,
still looking from your window
when the lawn has gone completely into shadow,
when you understand what small purchases
may be made that will suffice
and the great flap of your ear
hears, muffled and off key,
a little tune begin, whistling in your dark.
It's one of the citizens, alone and out late,
bucking himself up,
accompanied by the tattoo
of the battle hymn of the heart.

∂ᔥ Hamilton, Never President

You'll do for a six-pack and change.
Strange, you're most representative
of the people. The wide boulevards
outside The Treasury are pleasant with jalopies.
It is a Sunday afternoon
and the couple near the second street lamp
are from Ohio, stout Methodists,
who just this morning before they got on their touring clothes,
the brown suit and the flowering paradise dress,
were taken with middle-aged passion
and he entered her from behind as both looked out
on the trees in blossom, oh yes it is spring Alexander,
and you're seeing it too.
Butterflies are stitching from flower to flower
as though making homespun needlepoint slogans
to hang all around your porticos.

∂ᔥ Twenty Questions

Just to the left of Jackson's head
a citizen has written OK, OK
as if our seventh president were, what?
resigned to his high, thick collar
and swirling, rakish hair?
Or maybe this was a note, unreserved,
passed in church, a message so urgent
it couldn't wait for less valuable paper.

But how do we read it—
affirmation? grim acceptance?
Is it a double question, OK? OK?
Or a question and an answer, OK? OK.
Or maybe two answers, OK. OK.
Here, in the republic with its Federal
Reserve System, its well-regulated military
and its three branches of government,
how do we read it?

❧ Fifty-fifty

"What would it take,
just for once,
to get you to shut up
about responsibility?
What would a little peace cost?
I mean just close your mouth,
you know I used to love your mouth,
and just not talk,
not ask,
not beg of me
not utter a goddamn word.
Yes, I said utter.
I uttered utter.
What I owe you!
Am I owed?
Am I owed nothing?
Here, here, take it.

Just shut up and take it.
If you ask me,
Old Grant looks just as drunk."

    Poor Ben's Almanac

This little broadside contains
the only kind of advice
we really want to receive,
offered by the Treasurer of the United States
and the Secretary of the Treasury,
the spire of Independence Hall separating
IN GOD from WE TRUST.
It's about 12 minutes after five here
and all upper case, the trees officially green.
Two gentlemen stand off from each other
in front of the main entrance.
They don't seem to notice that the numeral 100
pegs each corner or that the earth beneath them
proclaims ONE HUNDRED DOLLARS,
the sky above THE UNITED STATES OF AMERICA
and beyond the sky a simple border like chair rail.
They don't seem to notice this.
It might rain though there's no clouds.
The two men go on about their business,
early to bed and early to rise.

STATE BIRD

The feet of the state bird were used at the throat of the ceremonial robes
of natives, oracular clasp at the voice box,

shouts to Walt Whitman, his yawp cranked, hip hop language line, the
stuffed state bird wired to his wrist for a portrait,

John James Audubon, deadly painter, still life of the state bird recorded,
male and female in the Eden his bird shot preserved,

the state bird in the state tree like a brilliant idea in a green mind,
Democracy in the cerebrum of a slaveowner, pink Wallace Stevens deep
in the wood of his office reading actuary tables,

on the windshield, the state bird shit of the state bird,

for this line I have imagined Emily Dickinson needed to keep a linen
handkerchief embroidered with the state bird in the third drawer of her
bureau and daily she studied it, her rapid eyes like frightened beads,

in a diary entry of Shiloh, of Antietam, of the Wilderness, of Gettysburg,
of Cold Harbor, no mention of the state bird,

unable to access file <statebird.gov>,

the state bird was a compromise in the bicameral legislature,

how would you like to wake up to find your talons stuffed with arrows
and laurel, sporting a Yankee Doodle breastplate and a beak full of
Latin,

and now the state bird comes to my feeder; I have used his hunger to
gain a pleasant glimpse and he is fed,

William Carlos Williams once sutured up a state bird, performing the
surgery wearing only an old housecoat and his horn-rim spectacles,

Teddy Roosevelt kept a state bird caged and fed it with tweezers,

thirty-one state birds were approved by voice vote,

in a flit across the road, this state bird found the state's official
protection to be no match for the bumper of a late model Caprice and
he has since merged with the macadam in such a flattened form as to
become an actual icon if such a thing is possible which it seems to be
here on Alternative 58 just shy of Dudley,

the state bird is non-migratory,

there was discussion and amendment to the motion of the state bird,

Robert Frost was a dead eye with a sling shot and once killed and
plucked a state bird only to have it fly off later in a poem,

the state bird must consume one-third its weight in insects each day; on
warm summer afternoons the bugs are like nuggets of melting caramel,

Sylvia Plath hated the state bird, hated state, hated the word bird, hated
its red wings and their excitable flutter,

68 yea, 32 nay,

Thomas Jefferson taught a state bird to mimic the opening bars of a
Copland fanfare,

in local news, a Duplin man was fined $200 and court costs for killing a
state bird; the man claimed that he was not intending to kill the bird
but merely to shoot up his neighbor's unsightly piece of lawn art,

the state bird prefers the understory, its own kind, its actual foot on an
actual limb, its local claws, local wings, local beak and local song.

DENSE FOG IN WHICH I MISS THE EASTERN SEABOARD'S LARGEST FLAG FLYING OVER A TOYOTA DEALERSHIP OFF I-95 NEAR WASHINGTON, D.C.

White night,
distance is done in.

Is this Heaven,
this cloud come to ground?

Our lights
are two short sticks;

they cannot reach
to tap the ground.

Our velocity's
an edge, a ledge.

In here is risk.
Notice we slow only slightly.

Do I hear a horn,
a siren in this air raid?

Here's smoke from big guns;
we've been vaporized.

We plunge.
Where are we going

that we keep going
in this?

Muhammad Ali couldn't
punch out of this sogging.

General MacArthur's howitzers
couldn't hammer it.

Nixon couldn't lie this away,
nor Clinton nor Bush.

I can see no Edward Hopper
billboards for Calvin Klein.

Great Nature has lowered
the curtain on commerce.

I am mole to this tunnel.
Even the CIA is blind here.

Wait, Elvis is singing to Ella.
I'll follow that. No, it's gone.

I tap my brakes.
What might be ahead

is blank, a history
to be written.

The first woman president
is invisible on the shoulder.

My _____ville, my _____ton,
my _____boro have vanished.

This is aftermath,
mushroom cloud come down.

Where has the country gone?
Where the vets at the VFW?

Where the ruckus at Woodstock?
And the Lions and Bengals and Bears?

Please give us back our lynchings,
our oil wars, our dead rivers.

We'll take Enron and Exxon
for one more cup of joe

at the diner of our pork-barrel,
pot-bellied, waddling democracy.

Ah, there, thank God,
a mudflap with a busty

silver silhouette.
We are saved.

And now the sun,
a platinum disc

on the office wall
of the big boss exec

is burning through
and thank you, Mr. Postman,

for our speed limits,
our exit ramps and cloverleaves,

our vision, our miles of asphalt
returned to us.

THE ACCIDENT

THE ACCIDENT

She couldn't bring herself
         to fill out the life insurance forms.

Bring herself.

From where she sat now she could see clouds,
         the billow of them.

It could be like drawing she thought.

The work of the pen.

Life insurance. Sure, right.

Fill out the billow.

The last thing he ate was a peach.

What a pretty thought. Fill out.

Bring herself.
         The way she felt at the roadside. Brought.

Not traveled to. Appeared.

That spot, that random roadside nowhere spot, became a location.

There was no distance to the clouds. Fill out.

Forms. Blanks.

A line. A shiver. So hot it was cold.

The young cop. She wanted to hear her name.

For someone to say it.

Not traveled to. There were clouds. Blanks.

Not fill out. Fill in.

Failure to Yield

For Henry Sink

The day's fuse is lit,
seventy-eight degrees at eight-thirty.

Numbers as words
and the sky a blank blue.

This is what is meant
by "the kingdom of heaven."

One minus one.
Susan was able to tell without crying

how Henry felt his worries
were behind him

when he was riding his motorcycle.
The truck's driver was charged with "failure to yield."

Words as numbers.
Another blue-sky day.

Eighty-two at eight fifty-nine.

1953 – 2007.

Tires

Exhausted, they've been tossed behind
the garage. They've gotten nowhere.
Sure, they made tracks. They got
around. They were once in the service
of the Prince of Ohio. But no, they did
not answer opportunity's knock. And
now, now, they slosh if tipped. Water
runs their rut. They breed blood-feeders.
They wail for their fate. O. O. O. O.

NOW AND IN OUR
TIME OF NEED

Crows know the give and go.

They imprint like words on the sky's blue page.

They fly through the pine stand like a sentence.

If we could read that swift progress,
that syntax,

if we could follow its logic,

if we could with the mind's eye
discern the tone of its locution—

see how it moves through the boughs,
that thought, that flock,

that going that is the way the mind moves,
that prayer flashing in the understory—

if only we could.

Clamor

On my afternoon walk I hear a pileated woodpecker
knocking on the door of a dead tree.

What welcome for such a visitor,
rapping on the upright lifeless wood,

coming to call on the delicious grubs?
The little cousin of the Lord God bird

knock knocks on my afternoon walk.
Weeks later, we got notice that the funeral home

had taken an impression of his index finger
and now offered a charm bearing his print.

I imagined the concentration on the face
of the funeral home employee, lifting the dead hand,

the finger daubed with ink, and pressing it to a pad.
He wanted to get a good impression of the whorl,

the unique cosmos on the end of the finger
for a silver pendant the daughter will wear.

There is a knock on a door by an unseen hand.
No one answers.

Instructions for Afterward

Shine and sleep and hum
and drum your mute fingers on the table.

Say of someone dead
a particular tree they were fond of.

Say of an empire
its contributions to the art of baking.

Secret. Sing words
that are not the words to the song.

Wrong the weather
and throw rocks at a sign of the times.

When you leave the body
don't be afraid to notice how the tongue lolls

from the slack mouth.
We are more than half slouch

and droop and sag.
Love our unbecoming.

WHEN YOU PRAY
DO NOT PRAY FOR

1. The sick. They have their own problems.

2. Any small birds, raptors above them, cats with their accurate teeth.

3. Desperate individuals. Give them money.

4. The balm a full moon offers its given night.

5. Luck. Never. Better to daub a sore with the essential oils of "You better believe it."

6. A hillside in Independence, Virginia. Its sable grass like fur.

7. Any sort of understanding whatsoever.

8. Nevertheless. Nevertheleast. Nevermore.

9. The items on the surgeon's desk, to rearrange them.

10. Sleep. Its old pony-skin trunk and yellowed sheaves of freight manifests.

Volunteer

She finds a cicada husk fastened to
a tree trunk. It's translucent, brown,
the exact shape of the insect before it
climbed into flight. The shell is split
down the back. It clings to the tree. Even
when she nudges it, it will not let go.

She comes every Monday around 9 to
weed the memorial garden, rake, prune,
whatever needs doing. She doesn't
believe, but it's a lovely garden and
near to her place. She can walk. Ashes
have been scattered here. Mondays the
building is empty until about 11, when
one of the ministers comes in to check
for messages. By the time she is finished
there will be a dark crescent moon—
someone?—under each finger's nail.

C. S. Lewis Goes to the Zoo

"When we set out I did not believe that Jesus is the
Son of God and when we reached the zoo I did."

The dung on the concrete floors,
the gravel paths from cage to cage,

the shadow of the jaguar, pacing as it paced.
It was deranged, I believe, with captivity.

The monkeys would not look at us
or the children tethered to their shrieks.

The placid rhinos were like furniture
and the elephants ill-fitted to their skin.

Suddenly, I knew that I was being kept out
not they in.

PROOF

PROOF

In the attic, I'm like a bad idea, a
headache. Am I not lordly? There are
stacks of boxes jammed with everything we
don't need but have saved. Their dust is
on my fingers. I will transfer it later.

This is the past with its old books about
God and cursive. If I could believe my
hands I would leave.

Through the small, milky window, I see
a girl I don't know. She's come into the
backyard and is stepping carefully among
the windfalls under the pear tree. She
seems to know they are spiked with bees.

EARLY WALK,
EVERYTHING TOUCHED WITH
DO NOT TOUCH

Sun-stung, the hoary grass breathes.
You can see it exhale.

The mailbox smokes,
night's black frozen loaf.

I quicken, feet feeling
held to a fire

and pick up the news.
The doorknob burns

my ungloved hand.
This cold is not. It's hot

and has scorched my ears.
Inside, the cold comes alive.

I've brought it in.
It caresses my neck.

My skin sings,
growing cold as it warms.

I blush. Its attentions
are not unwanted.

My white cup steams,
the chill at its lip,

good little death
coming back into my body.

MOTORCYCLE

rides in with the gospel, the part after the resurrection where
Jesus says "Don't touch me, I'm not ascended yet"

the crumpled hulk of it, back in the shed where it always
stayed, waiting for Henry

earthbound, as close as we get to flying

Tom hauling his thrill, his absolute earthly joy, to the dirt
track in Gallipolis, Ohio, that state with its own two wheels

on the way to the zoo, the wind of its own making raking
C.S. Lewis in the midst of conversion

it is an elegant solution, if a plus b equals c, c is the blur of
the landscape in the midst of its conversion

the jacket, the chaps, the skin of other creatures got on in
what his mother called the get-up

it goes by leaning

it's not point a to point b, it's the line described, the work of
the wrist

along the parkway, the yellow leaves, the near black-red of the
sweetgum danced in its aftermath

and Thomas put his finger in the wound, that lush rushing, the wind
   of that wonder

kick stand, a jaunty pose, a Whitman, one of the guys

the ride an unraveling, a holding on to let go

Henry would get it out of the shed not to go somewhere in particular

the helmet with its notions of nothing

it is nearly all engine, smacked up now, its rev run out

Tom rode a Ducati on the Grecian switchbacks, O Wheeled One,
   Far Seer, Fleetness, wing him yet

the uncertainty principle, you can know speed or location, not both

on the side of the road in South Carolina, before the emergency
   airlift his breathing changed when she spoke of her love

a wisp of blue smoke, if you looked quickly, when it cranked.

DEAD RECKONING

I used to think he willed the rabbits to be
just where he looked.
In the fields he paid fierce attention,
would see them sitting in their tight tucks
under honeysuckle before they spooked.

He said you had to look for their eyes,
the black blaze of their watching,
his hot search for their gaze.

Then he would take their heads off clean
with his 12 gauge.
You probably don't know how hard that is,
a gun that could make a hole the size of a bowling ball
and he could, close range, take their teacup heads off
and leave their bodies unmarred.

Children with good parents get a false idea of God.
They misunderstand prayer and believing and practice,
the roar of the gun, the plush limp bodies.
I would carry them in my hunting coat,
the last warmth of them in the pouch at the small of my back.

In Song the Words are Fruit, in Prayer Blight

Butterflies drop-stitch to the butterfly bush,
yellow hinge, black hinge,
                    freed from the door of perception.

Spurt of wren flight out of the boxwood.
The morning idles, engines trimmed,
cicadas trolling the understory.

Time is taking its time for the moment.
Nothing doing though I think a pepper
is ripening on the pepper plant.

Then I notice the slow muscle of him
climbing the dogwood, yard-long,
                    inching his way
toward the cardinal nest.

He'll unhinge his jaw if need be.
What is more silent than an egg?

He'll take each one into his mouth,
thread himself with them,
                    his body bulge strung.

If he's grateful I don't know it
when he lets himself back down noiselessly.

≥∜

Hard by joe-pye and jimson weed,
in the scrick-scrack of the ditch trash,
                                        a cross,
some left-over slats knocked together,
painted white, a bouquet of plastic flowers beside.

Someone died here, perhaps of excessive speed,
perhaps nodding into the last nap,
                                    and now nothing is more silent
in sad mute elegy than plastic flowers

and the slipshod cross that all afternoon
keeps driving itself into the earth.

≥∜

The night is body temperature.
                            Full moon glints the nail heads
in the backyard picket fence.
                                Trees glide in the orb's good graces.
Is there anything more quiet than moonlight?
Slats and shadows of slats, that bright a night,
rungs the light has laid down.

Every Head Bowed,
Every Eye Closed

The Hindu-turned-Christian wept in our hot little church.
We loved the curiosity of him, exotic as sandalwood, crying
for our hometown Jesus.

"Lord," the earnest young man prayed before the meal, "Lord,
we come to you today...." He called on God by name eleven
times, like a well-trained salesman with a client.

A yellow leaf unlatches. Later, it will skirr along the
macadam in the afterwind of a motorcycle.

"We pray that our leaders will have the courage of their
convictions and that our men and women in arms will be
safe and will return to us, their loving families."

The caterpillar does not merely sprout wings and grow
legs. The pupa actually passes through a liquid stage before
solidifying into an entirely new creature. With iridescent
blue wings.

He sorted the letters from an old calf-skin trunk, letters his
mother wrote to this father away at the war. That's the way
it was said—away at the war. "I pray for you nightly and ask
God to shield you, to lay his mantle on you." She had a way
with words.

The moonlight made a blue path on the water, unwalkable.

"Every head bowed, every eye closed," intoned the hawkeyed evangelist. "I see someone on the verge of accepting Jesus as her personal savior."

Orange, ocher, parchment brown. The leaves littered the water. Drifted. Slow kaleidoscope.

There was a great rushing of wind and people began to speak in tongues. Tongues not of this land. Perhaps not of this world.

The light, yes the light, was yellow and moved in the understory, a love-struck young girl. Her eyes brimmed like pools.

When the black man from cultural services began to sing "He Touched Me" in my father's hospital room, my father began to cry, quietly. My mother took his hand.

The hawk flurried the song birds from the feeder and then perched on its wrought iron arch a moment. It surveyed the yard then rowed away to another hunt, another miss or a kill.

The evangelist mopped his face with his handkerchief. It looked to have been pressed before it soaked up his sweat and tears. There was one more soul that wanted to come to the altar.

The motorcycle, that thrilling contraption, leaned in the curves and made a wind with its speed. Ah, the risk of it, the ride a flying.

Lord, I... Lord, let... Lord, give... Lord, please....

Lord, the pewter rain plucks the surface of the lake. To the lake, Lord, the rain is admitted.

EXCEPT

Early April and suddenly
flurries are mixing with bloom fall.

I'm on my way to a friend's third wedding
and two seasons are dancing together across the windshield.

What shield from the wind, nothing's push,
not-here's nod in the trees, do we ever have?

White in white are the vows we make,
the blossom *yes* of them sailing with each crystal *no*.

I will try to love you and you me, we'll see.
Two seasons are in a waltz, one, two, three.

Spring is not birth and winter death.
That's our little myth.

Snow and bloom are ready companions,
a marriage of possibilities in wind,

that buoyant flow, that what not what.
By noon, brief litter, the snow is gone

except where it lingers in the shadows of cedars,
those tear-shaped trees.

Go in Fear of Abstractions

It's summer now.

But I'm thinking snow,
the snows of yesteryear

with three crows gliding in.

As they alight
Chinese characters form against the snow's rice paper.

Wellness. Beauty. The Divine.

They are there so suddenly,
blindingly black on white.

But now no snow.
No snow now.

Answer

Morning Prayer

A kid has left a tricycle
at the edge of my yard.

A tricycle has such an expectant look.
Hey, I'm ready to go.

Has anyone noticed I'm red?
And have a bell?

And handlebar tassels!
What could possibly call

a life away from this contraption?
Questions are such three-legged things,

sturdy, upright,
standing on their own.

They've got anxious pedals,
and someone gone off somewhere.

And silent bells burring
at the edge of the yard.

⚡ *Prayer at Midday*

I'm going to sit out here
until I get some discernment.

Nothing yet.
Maybe I should eat something.

Maybe a spoonful of yogurt
is all that's between me and enlightenment.

Inside I've left the radio on.
A rumble of music I can't really make out.

Rock? Country? Celtic Fusion?
Hard to tell through the wall.

But music without doubt.
Without doubt.

⚡ *Evening Prayer*

Someone is using the PA
at the high school football field.

I can hear the giant grumblings
from the back porch.

It's as if someone is translating
billboards into a dead language.

I can't tell what he's announcing,
what event is being narrated.

It's a quarter mile through the trees.
Long pauses while something happens

I can only hear tell of.
Such graceful movements garbled.

When it ends it will be a while
before I can be sure.

Now Not Now

It's our personal mythology
that we know the moment our son was conceived.
We could tell you if we told such things.

It's a fact
that I know the exact moment my father died.
The four of us at his bedside.

If I told such things
the sparrows this morning seem to be ransacking the boxwood,
little handfuls of flutter spurting in and out
of the fragrant shrub.

Mythical creature the two of us made,
half one thing, half another.

A vein pulsed weakly in his neck
even when the ICU nurse said, "He's gone."

Afterwards, we heard deer grazing
through the screen windows of the tourist cabin.
It sounded like whispering.

HERE I AM, LORD

The ribbed black of the umbrella
is an argument for the existence of God,

that little shelter
we carry with us

and may forget
beside a chair

in a committee meeting
we did not especially want to attend.

What a beautiful word, "umbrella."
A shade to be opened.

Like a bat's wing, scalloped.
It shivers.

A drum head
beaten by the silver sticks

of rain,
and I do not have mine,

and so the rain showers me.

THE FEATHER AGAINST WHICH
MY HEART WILL
BE WEIGHED

The crow feather I found was not an idea.
The crow feather was a black slash on the green lawn.
It was a way of counting. One. One.

The crow feather seemed to be waiting for me.
It rested, abided, as though placed just so
for the one time I would walk to its threshold.

I believe the crow feather when it is in my hand.
I know that it is a feather in my hand,
black quill, inkless, for writing out the gospel.

GOING

To seep
would be my way.

If I were a river,
I'd be trickly,

ankle-deep
and summer slow.

I'd rather be
a creek than

an Ohio
with barges

on my shoulders,
wake-foamed.

It's better
to be cunning,

creeping water,
to sneak and sop

moss beds,
to dampen sand

and be siphoned
by butterflies,

to rise in reeds
like music

in flutes,
a ribbon

capable of glint.

MOSES

Some bush is letting go
its next season,

thistledown or fluff
from milkweed pods

but I don't know
the name of these,

like the soul, singular
and plural, snow

we'd think
were it colder,

or white gnats,
a dismantling cloud

and everyone going
about their business

as if seed
and seedtime

were not
swarming.

My Hole's Got a Bucket in It

It's a galvanized tin bucket
down there at the bottom of the excavation.
It's the kind of bucket you think of
when you hear the word "bucket."
It's the idea of bucket,
tipped on its side, so it holds nothing.
Its something has spilled.
Or maybe it held nothing when it tipped
and its nothing spilled.
A portable hole, a bucket
can be filled.

My hole is the beginning
of a room, a new room,
an absence the start of presence,
more residence.
But a room is a sort of hole,
to be filled with valuables,
loved ones. And yet
the room is never completely filled,
something, someone, is always missing,
the bucket, overturned, down there now
in the hole that contains it.

THE VISITOR

His death is getting a haircut, just a trim today Lou.

His death has a question about last Sunday's sermon.

His death hums, a tune from the upright in the old parlor.

His death smiles at the light streaming there.

His death traded cars last month.

His death is looking for arrowheads along the river bank.

His death waits while the oil's changed.

His death counted doves on the electric line. Five.

His death checks the rearview.

His death worries the wedding band around the ring finger.

His death paces, floorboards creaking in the living room.

THE ROOM

One way or another, we must all leave
I said to a room, a room empty of people,
save for me. There were two doors to the room,

ample avenues of departure. A small town.
A family. A faith. A marriage. A career.
The dailiness of days' work done for years.

We are leaving even as we speak I said to no one
in the room with me. To whom did I speak?
To ones already left, though left can mean

both to remain and to depart? Dearly departed,
you remain here with me in this empty room,
room enough for you, empty in my aching thought.

Leavings are that scatter, those remaining remnants,
our language littered with what can't be gotten rid of,
our thoughts, our bodies ghosted, the leavings remaining.

Acknowledgments

Thanks to the following magazines and their editors for first printing
these poems:

ABZ "Motorcycle"

Boulevard "Failure to Yield"

Cincinnati Review "Going"

Crazyhorse "A Marriage Must Be Worked At,"
"Be Good To Yourself" and "Go in Fear of Abstractions"

Field "Crows as the Figure of Disease," "Early Walk,
Everything Touched with Do Not Touch,"
"Federal Reserve Notes," "Fourth Hour of the
Afternoon," "Three Dogs as the Figure of Death"
and "Tires"

Image "In Song the Words Are Fruit, In Prayer Blight"

Iron Mountain Review "Every Head Bowed, Every Eye Closed"

Mudfish "State Bird"

New Letters "The Deer"

Poetry "Don't Complain," "Here I Am, Lord" and
"Take Comfort Where You Can"

Poetry Northwest "Proof"

Slate "The Room"

Smartish Pace	"The Visitor"
Southern Poetry Review	"Answer"
The New Republic	"The Feather Against Which My Heart Will Be Weighed"
The Sun	"Instructions for Afterward"

Much thanks to Michael McFee for his insights on the individual poems and the manuscript as a whole. Such a good reader is a tremendous gift.

And my deep gratitude to the families of Henry Sink and Tom Andrews. Thank you for sharing them with me.

Other books from Tupelo Press

See our complete backlist at www.tupelopress.org